MW01596444

Battling Demons

A Memoir of Mental Growth

Battling Demons

A Memoir of Mental Growth

By Marcus Whitley

First Print Edition. 2024

Written by Marcus Whitley
Edited by Lisa Howard

ISBN EBOOK   979-8-218-41851-9
ISBN PRINT   979-8-218-37006-0

Library of Congress Control Number: 2024902446

For any inquiries regarding this book, please email:
iammarcuswhitley@gmail.com

www.thehardestchoices.com

This book is dedicated to my son

Melo Lee

I pray every day that these demons aren't
hereditary and won't be passed down to you. I don't
ever want you to live with this kind of pain. I tried
my best to internalize them so you'd never have to
see me suffer. I know you will battle demons of your
own throughout your life and I will always be with
you. I just hope you will never have to face mine.
All I want is for you to grow into the man I raised
you to be. I know you will do remarkable things.
Everything you need to be great is already in you.
Don't ever wait for opportunities to come to you.
Kick down the door and make opportunities
available! There are no excuses if you want
something bad enough. I love you more than life
itself. Always!

Not every day is going to be a good day, but even through the bad days, you can find some good. You just have to stay positive and be optimistic.

Table of Contents

Introduction

Everyone has demons they battle on a daily basis. Some are worse than others and have a stronger influence. Some aren't able to be explained or diagnosed, so they get overlooked. Some go unnoticed for so long that they become a part of you.

There are many ways that demons can affect you and take control of your mind and body. These demons can be emotions like guilt, fear, anger, or hopelessness, or they can be memories of times you failed or were hurt. They can be thoughts like *"It's too hard"* or *"I'm not good enough"* or *"I'm going to fail."* It's possible you can become so consumed by these thoughts and emotions that you lose yourself and may never be able to find yourself again.

One of the hardest things to do for many people is to ask for help. Whether it's pride that gets in the way, fear of rejection, being laughed at, or being too embarrassed it's not easy to ask for help. What's even harder is admitting to yourself that you need help.

I wrote this book to bring awareness to these demons and show others that it's okay to talk about their demons. Trying to hide them or bottle them up can be harmful in all kinds of ways: mentally, physically, and emotionally. All my life, I denied that my demons existed and I bottled up all my emotions. I think I was too prideful to believe that anything was "wrong" with me. I was too scared to ask about what was going on and too embarrassed to ask for help. I didn't know *how* to ask, and I felt like even if I did, who would listen? I felt like people would judge me, call me crazy, or just laugh at me.

In my experience, talking to a therapist hasn't worked, either. My mind moves faster than I can ever get the words out, which means I can never say what I'm trying to say. That's when I become frustrated and shut down. Once that happens, I'm not able to process anything at that time. There's no telling how long I might get lost in that state of mind. It becomes a waiting game, one that causes me to miss out on all kinds of things because all I want to do is isolate myself.

But writing has always been an outlet and a strength for me. I find peace when I write—it helps me express myself more than I could in any other way. It's therapeutic and helps me understand myself a little bit better. This book is my therapy—writing it has given me the power to face my demons. I hope to inspire others to find ways of facing their own demons.

Follow me through each chapter as I uncover my demons and shine a light on the fact they exist. Every day is a struggle and I learned that if I wanted it to change—I had to be the change.

Surrounded By Demons

Demons don't have a physical form—they don't live in my closet or under my bed like we believed monsters did when we were kids. The demons that I live with are inside my head; they control most of my thoughts, feelings, and sometimes even my actions. They overpower me and make me feel helpless over my own being. It's not like the movies where they haunt me or influence me to do anything—rather, they simply take over my mind and dictate what I'm doing or not doing today. This has made life very difficult and unpredictable. After all, I never know what mental state I'll be in when I wake up or which demons I'll face each day.

It's never easy pretending to be okay when I'm not. Hiding my thoughts and emotions has become normal for me because I struggle with talking about them. I've grown numb to the pain and have learned to live with it as well as I can. It seems like a one-sided battle that can't be won, yet I refuse to give up.

Childhood

To start from the beginning, I'm the oldest of five kids. I have four half-siblings. We're all mixed, but I'm the only one who's Black and Italian—my brothers and sisters are mixed with Spanish. I've never been too close to any of them, but I think that's because I'm so much older than they are. Don't get me wrong, we all love each other to death. We're just not around each other and we didn't talk to each other that much.

By the time they were all born, I already had one foot on the pavement. Being a role model was something I never imagined I would have to be. I was a child but also the only man in the house. All I could think about was money. We didn't live in the safest neighborhood, although as a kid, I didn't understand what that meant. My friends were my friends and we hung out every day outside.

My life has always been a struggle. It's never been easy and nothing about it has been fair. Growing up with nothing, my father leaving, being bullied because I'm Black…on top of that, all my life I was looked at as being a failure. The hate has always outweighed the love, but still, that never made me bitter. However I guess, it did make me bottle up my feelings and disconnect from my emotions.

But who am I to complain? Everyone has problems and things they deal with. Nobody wants to hear me crying about it. Even if I did, it wouldn't change anything. Maybe that's why for as long as I can remember, I've been anti-social. People always assume I'm shy, but that's not it at all—most of the time, I'm in my head and I just don't want to talk or like to talk. It's hard to open up because when I did in the past, it didn't go well. I have trust issues and trauma because of that. I'm not sure if I'll ever be able to trust anyone again.

Nightmares

I've also been having nightmares on and off ever since I was a kid. They're always different, but play out the same way in the end: I would die, and each time in a different way. No matter what I do the outcome never changes. These nightmares are so vivid and detailed that I believe they're real. I wake up covered in sweat, checking my body to make sure I'm okay or I would jump straight out of bed with my fists clenched, ready to fight. When I was younger, I would sleep with a knife or a gun under my pillow, thinking that someone was going to try to kill me while I was sleeping. Those nightmares made me paranoid.

There's been times I've stayed awake all night just because I didn't want to go to sleep. That was a battle I rarely won but, not winning didn't stop me from trying. Why can't I have normal nightmares about monsters or something scary like other kids? Why do I always have to die? I've always wondered if people can control what they dream about, but that doesn't seem like a possibility.

Insecurities

Anything I've ever gotten in life, I've had to work hard for. I take pride in that. I've always been the type of person who has to finish anything I start. Maybe it's the obsessive-compulsive disorder I have, but when I become focused on something, I create this kind of tunnel vision. Once I'm done, though, that's another story. That's when the doubt and the questions come in. I start to feel like no matter what I do, no matter how hard I work or what I accomplish, it's never enough. It'll never be good enough. *I'll* never be good enough. There are so many other people out there who are better than me and have already done exactly what I'm doing better than how I'm doing it. That aggressive animal instinct I initially had disappears, and suddenly I'm not enough. Once that hunger is gone, it's hard to get back. Sometimes impossible.

Depression

I feel like depression plays a major part in my life. It's one of my biggest battles and something I've struggled with my entire life. I still don't know where it stems from, but I'm guessing there's a long list of things to pick from: countless traumatic experiences, neglect, being hated and bullied, poverty, being told I'm a failure and that I'll never be good enough, and so many other things. All I know how to do is shut down and push people away. I don't want to talk to anyone or do anything—I just want to be left alone. It's not healthy, but I don't know any other way of dealing with these issues.

Part of my depression stems from the fact that I feel like nobody will understand me or what I'm going through. Anyone I talk to will judge me or think I'm crazy, so the only thing I can do is keep everything to myself. But little by little, I can feel it killing me inside. Being anti-social has become so normal for me that even having conversations with my own family is hard to do. When I lost touch with my emotions, I lost a part of myself. That void became filled with all of these things and made me unrecognizable—even to myself.

Anxiety

Depression isn't the only thing I've been struggling with. I battle so many demons on a daily basis that my anxiety has been through the roof. It causes me to have panic attacks and be even more short-tempered than usual. That's never been fun to deal with. Anxiety makes me not like being around people even more than I already don't like to. I hate being in large crowds and feel uncomfortable whenever I do have to be in them. I hate being in small crowds, too. I hate having any attention focused on me and I feel awkward whenever I'm complimented for anything. It's ironic because my passions and the field of work I'm in force me to put myself into those kinds of situations, so learning to open up more is necessary. If I don't find ways to adapt and adjust, I won't be able to do what I do and be good at it. I love what I do more than I hate my anxiety, so I refuse to let it stop me. It's not easy, but what other choice do I have? If I don't pick myself up and push forward, who will?

Anger

Demons appear in so many different forms, that it's hard to notice them most of the time. What's even worse is when I'm fighting with myself or with someone else who's trying to point out that they see something is wrong. These demons know how to manipulate my mind into believing that everything is normal and that I don't have a problem. That causes me to get angry at others and become defensive for saying I do have a problem.

Nobody wants to believe that they have an addiction or struggle with mental health. I know I don't! Every day I look in the mirror and tell myself that I'm good. I'm not sure if I'm trying to convince myself or asking myself if I am. Part of me believes that saying those things could make a difference, but another part of me feels like I'm lying to myself.

At this point, I don't know what's right and what's wrong, what's real and what's not. I just try to make it through each day and hope that I won't fail.

A Recurring Dream

I woke up gasping for breath, feeling like I had just emerged from being underwater. Sweat was dripping down my face and my pillow was soaked. I could feel my heart racing like it was about to burst out of my chest. I started checking my body and taking deep breaths—inhaling through my nose and exhaling through my mouth—as I tried to slow my heart rate. I sat up, pulled the blanket off, and felt chills run through my body.

"How could I be sweating if it's this cold?" I thought. I looked out the window and noticed that it was still dark outside. Something didn't feel right. I prayed I wasn't getting sick. COVID-19 had been around for a while, and many people have died because of it.

I stood up and quickly became nauseous. I felt like I had a hangover but I hadn't had a drink in months. I lost my balance and fell back onto the bed. The dizziness became too much; I just had to wait it out.

Moments later, I attempted to stand up and walk to the bathroom. I was still shaking off the dizziness. I looked behind the shower curtain and saw an empty shower. Maybe it's because I was locked up before or maybe I'm just paranoid but I always feel like someone could hiding behind the curtain or around the corner and might jump out and kill me if I don't check. The feeling has caused me to always have my guard up, even when I'm alone. I've gotten so used to it that it has become a daily routine. As a child, I never believed in monsters, but with the things I've done in my life, I've become scared of myself. I turned on the water to wash my face as I looked in the mirror, trying to find a small piece of good in me somewhere in my reflection. But, all I saw was a blank, emotionless face and a dark shadow in the background. I don't even recognize myself anymore. Not to mention, my shadow doesn't even resemble my physical stature at all—it's like I'm being followed around by someone or some*thing* else's shadow.

After brushing my teeth and getting dressed, I headed out the door to go to work. It was still early and I wanted to get a workout in before the two training sessions I had scheduled.

When I pulled into the back parking lot, I saw a few junkies hanging out, which wasn't surprising—they're always looking for an open door late at night or early in the morning so that they can get high inside one of the buildings.

I pulled out a razor blade that I kept in my glovebox and slipped it into my pocket. As I walked past them to get to the door, I gripped the blade tightly in case one of them made any sudden movements toward me. They didn't. I entered the building and locked the door behind me.

Now it was just me and the dimly lit hallway and the three flights of stairs leading up to the gym. Even though the door was locked, I was still holding onto the razor blade and looking around every corner. I stopped every few steps to listen for noises and heard nothing except my own breathing. Maybe it was the way some of the lights were flickering, but there seemed to be a shadowy figure at the top of the stairs. I pulled out my phone and shined the flashlight at the top of the stairs as I continued walking up to the fourth floor. The shadow vanished. As I looked around, I didn't notice mine, either. I brushed it off and went into the gym.

Finishing my workout and the two training sessions had me feeling better both mentally and physically. I was able to clear my head and get a good sweat; I started planning for a productive day as I headed home to shower and change. I grabbed a box of my book *Both Sides of the Street: Choices & Consequences* and put it in the car, thinking about a few different spots and youth programs where I wanted to sell or donate the book.

With all the bad things I've done in my life, I hope to stop someone else from making those same choices. I know it won't save me; I don't expect it to. But it's about *their* future and offering *them* guidance. I'll never be able to escape my demons. I may be able to push things deep down and not open up to anyone else, but I can't lie to the man I see in the mirror. Or to the shadow that follows me around.

I feel like this shadow judges me every time I look in the mirror. It doesn't have a face, but I can feel it staring at me, and even though it's my own shadow, it always gives me an unsettling feeling. At times, I've thought the shadow could be connected to the random nausea and cold sweats that I get, but I don't see how a shadow could cause physical problems. It *has* definitely affected my mental state, though—and it feels like my mind has been playing tricks on me. Lately, I've been trying to block it out so that I don't feel like I'm going crazy.

After finishing, I packed the rest of the books into the car, I decided to get something to eat before I headed home for the night. It was already dark outside and starting to rain. I figured I'd stop and get some food when I got back into the city because it's cheaper than going to food spots on the highway.

I pulled off the downtown exit and noticed a few people scattered outside on the street. Between the rain and most of the street lights being out, the people were dark, blurry figures—I could only see shadowy outlines of what looked like people on the sidewalks. I kept driving and eventually pulled over at a gas station to fill up.

Something didn't feel right, but I ignored it because it seems like I always feel that way. There was no one in sight; no one even appeared to be inside the gas station. The rain was coming down so hard at that point, that I didn't even see my shadow on the ground.

I finished pumping the gas and ran back into the car. Drenched from the rain, I wiped the water off my face and started the car. I put my glasses back on, looked into the rearview mirror…and noticed my shadow behind me. But something was off. Sitting in the car, my shadow should've stretched from the front seat across the back seat, but it didn't—it was just sitting in the backseat.

Suddenly, I felt a cold chill on the back of my head. My body froze. I couldn't reach for the door handle or react; I was stuck. It took everything in me to turn my head. I heard a loud bang!

I woke up gasping for breath with sweat dripping down my face; I felt dizzy and nauseous. I grabbed my head in the hopes that it would stop spinning. The back of my head was throbbing.

I tried to lie down again, but I was wide awake and couldn't fall back asleep. Instead, I just stared at the ceiling and waited for the sun to rise.

Surviving The Nightmares

I've always thought of dreams as being an escape from reality, a fantasy created by your mind while your body sleeps, a fantasy where anything is possible. As a kid, I always loved the idea of having dreams and exploring my imagination. I wanted to be rich! I wanted to see space! I wanted to play in the NFL and do so many other things! When I was awake, I was able to imagine all of those great things—in fact, I would catch myself daydreaming a lot. But when I fell asleep, all of those dreams disappeared.

Every dream was cold and dark. They all took place on the same streets where I had spent my days. It seemed like those streets were where I was meant to be—I couldn't escape them. I lived in those streets. I ran them, I made money in them, some nights I slept in them, and I even went to prison because I couldn't leave them alone. It was a toxic relationship. I would say the streets are what made me a monster and caused a lot of my trauma but I'd be lying. There was something wrong with me way before that.

I was money-driven; I felt like I'd chosen the streets with good intentions. I left school so that I could work, but the money wasn't enough to make a significant difference or even allow me to take care of myself. The streets seemed like the answer—a way to make more money, which was all I wanted to do. In that sense, they were good. But the streets also painted a vivid and scary picture of what that lifestyle was all about.

The first nightmare I can remember happened when I was eleven years old. It was the first time I died in my dreams. I don't know why it happened, but I was never the same after that. That was when I became paranoid and began looking over my shoulder constantly. The dream seemed so real! I didn't know I was sleeping.

I was playing five-on-five football with some friends at our middle school. We were out on the open field. There were no field goals or extra points—every touchdown was 7 points. Down by one touchdown on our last drive of the game, we were moving the ball down the field. I was the fastest and most elusive running back our school had ever seen. That wasn't enough for our pickup game, though. We went four and out on our last drive and we lost by a touchdown.

It was a good game: I had two touchdowns and a lot of yards. We weren't playing on a real field, but I know I would've gotten around 100 yards the way I was running. I loved our games because it was good practice and helped us get better. It probably wasn't good or smart to be playing tackle football without a helmet or any pads, but we were young and having fun. Whenever the sun went down and the lights came on, we felt like we were on the big stage, like we were—playing in the NFL.

The other kids all had their bikes, but mine had a flat tire, so I had to walk home. A few of the kids who lived in the same direction as I did, rode slowly so that they wouldn't leave me behind. We were laughing and talking trash about the game on the way home, talking about how we would all make it to the NFL and what teams we would want to play for. Of course, I said I was going to be drafted by the New York Giants in the first round. That was my team! My dream! It was always on my mind. I said the first thing I would do is buy my mom a big house. I didn't care about buying anything for myself—I just wanted to play in the NFL and buy her that house.

The night sky seemed darker; most of the lights on the street had blown out and none of the houses along the street had their porch lights on. We started talking about how cheap the city was and how they couldn't even fix the street lights.

As we approached the stop sign at the corner, we heard a loud siren and saw flashing blue lights fly by us. I started laughing, thinking to myself that they were after somebody. Then it was suddenly quiet again. I looked back before I was about to cross the street and noticed that my friends were gone. I hadn't heard anyone pedaling, I didn't see anyone riding away; they just vanished.

Out of nowhere, someone yelled, "Freeze!" I panicked—I dropped the football and took off running across the street. It was so dark outside! I was trying my best not to trip. Why was I running? I hadn't done anything wrong. Or, had I done something wrong without knowing it? I didn't want to stop to find out. Once I was home and safe, I'd worry about those questions, but not while I was being chased.

Each time I looked back, I couldn't see anyone behind me or hear any other footsteps. All I heard was a voice yelling "STOP!" I jumped a fence and ran through someone's yard to get over to the next street.

As I stepped into the street, I felt something heavy hit me in the back of the head. Already tired from running, I quickly became dizzy and fell to the ground. I tried to get up so I could fight back, but I got kicked in the face. I felt the laces of a sneaker tear my skin on impact. It was a burning sensation that instantly made my eyes water.

I tried to look up to see who was attacking me, but my vision was blurry. All I could see was two shadowy figures—but it felt like four people hitting me. At that point, I was drifting in and out of consciousness and couldn't tell how many people were actually there.

I felt my ribs crack as they stomped on my side before kicking me in the stomach. Curling up into a ball to protect myself wasn't helping at all. It felt like hours went by, but really, after just a few moments, everything stopped. The night became quiet.

As I lay there, in a puddle of my own blood, gasping for breath, I heard a loud bang!

I jumped up, screaming and crying, still gasping for breath and frantically checking my face and body. Everything appeared to be okay physically, but it had all felt so real! I didn't know what to think or do. How was I supposed to feel? What had just happened? Why had it happened?

That was too traumatic for an eleven-year-old kid—or anyone—to have to experience.

That same nightmare has haunted me ever since. Maybe I had more nightmares than that when I was younger, but that recurring nightmare is the earliest and most graphic one I can remember.

Others came later that were just as traumatic. I never understood why I dreamed of myself dying so often. And not even just dying—but being murdered in every possible way. Each night would be different, yet I'd always remember every detail when I woke up. Did I ever have any good dreams? I wouldn't know, but I do know that I have no recollection of any.

I was scared to go to sleep, so I looked for any way to avoid it. I've always heard people say "I'll sleep when I'm dead" because there's so much they don't want to miss. But for me, I always felt like I would actually die if I went to sleep. It's never a good feeling when you don't know if you're going to wake up in the morning.

I've repeatedly seen myself being shot and left for dead in a place where my body wouldn't be found for months. Even when my body was recovered, I'd be unrecognizable. I've seen myself being stabbed and left lying on the ground, my throat slit, and choking on my own blood. I've seen myself thrown off the roof of a building. Even though it was a dream, it felt *so* real—I could feel it in my stomach like I was on a rollercoaster, as I fell to the ground.

I've felt every bone in my body and face shatter. I've seen myself being held underwater as the water filled up my lungs while I tried to scream for help. I've seen myself being shot in my car when someone ran up to the window, pointed a gun at me, and pulled the trigger. As I lay there dying, I saw the car being set on fire and my body burning. When I woke up, I could still smell flesh burning.

Through all of the nightmares I've had, two things have always been the same in every single one of them: I always die and I never see who kills me. All I ever see is a dark shadow shaped like a man, but with no face, no features, no identifiable clothing that stood out...just a shadow. I've tried to fight back; I've tried to run; I've tried to prepare myself so that I could do something to defend myself, but nothing changes the outcome. It's inevitable.

For a long time, I believed it was karma. Everything I've done and every mistake that I've made in my life was haunting me. The nightmares were far worse than anything I'd ever done in my life, but then again, karma doesn't play fair. What goes around comes back around twice as bad. At least, that's what I've always heard, and it has truly been my experience. But what if the nightmares aren't karma? What if they're just meant to scare me? Except what would they be scaring me away from? The nightmares started before I ever touched the streets.

I've always had a hustler's mindset. I don't mean that in an illegal way—I'm not talking about drugs. I would do things like go to the store to get penny candy and then sell it at school for more money. Or I'd sell my lunch tickets if I didn't want the lunch they were having that day.

Later on was more questionable, I started selling my Ritalin pills because I didn't want to take them. I refused to believe that there was anything wrong with me, so why would I take them? I knew a lot of people who did want Ritalin and loved prescription drugs. Why not make money instead of wasting pills that I wasn't going to take?

But still, even that was far off from all the nightmares I've been having. It just doesn't add up. I've *never* thought about suicide or killing anyone. All I've ever wanted to do was make money and help my family. I thought I had paid my dues when I went to prison. Isn't that enough? I don't understand why I still have these nightmares.

I'm grateful that I don't have them as much as I used to, but when will the nightmares finally stop?

Lost In My Thoughts

Dealing With Criticism

I've always been a confident and ambitious person. Whenever my mind is set on something, I get into grind mode; whatever it is, I have to see it through until the end. But somewhere along the line, my insecurities start to take over, and despite all the hard work I put in, I'm not able to feel accomplished or proud of myself even though I know you can't make everyone happy—no matter what you're trying to do, someone will always have something negative to say about it.

I post motivational videos on social media in the hopes of inspiring and brightening people's days, yet I get criticized regularly for it. My messages don't always please everyone, apparently, or maybe those viewers just feel like being negative and want to take it out on me. Most commonly, I get comments about how I look. I'm not sure why I get those types of comments when my appearance has nothing to do with the content of my videos, but okay.

For the longest time, I brushed off the criticism and didn't care what anyone said. My focus and hunger weren't allowing negativity to affect me in any way. As I got older, though, I started to question the negativity. Like, why is all the hard work I'm doing not good enough? What does the way I look have to do with the positive energy I'm trying to put out into the world? I started thinking about what I could do differently when deep down I knew I didn't need to change anything. Still, I often just get so stuck on the bad things that I don't let myself appreciate all the good things.

Fatherhood

Every time I look into my son's eyes, I see how much he resembles me—he's a lighter-skinned, blue-eyed version of me with a bigger personality and all of my traits. From the moment he was born, I couldn't look away. My eyes were glued to him as I watched the entire birth. That was when I knew I had to do more. It wasn't just about me anymore—now, I'm a father and everything that comes along with being a father.

That means I'm a provider, a protector, a role model, and everything else I need to be to prepare him for the world and make sure he'll be successful. He's already into sports, which I knew he would be because it runs in the family. Still, it makes me so proud to see him happy, healthy, and active!

He was so excited when I published my books. He was only two years old, yet he was running around the house and yelling, "Look, Dad's books!" To me, that felt like a bigger accomplishment than any of the successes my books have had or even *writing* the books. He loves coming out with me to promote them and sell copies. He's been my motivation and my biggest supporter. If it weren't for him, I don't know what I would be doing or where I would be in life right now.

When I look into my daughter's eyes, in contrast, I don't see myself looking back at me. She doesn't resemble me the way my son does because we're not biologically connected. I came into her life a little over a year after her father had passed away. It's been hard for both of us, but fortunately, she fell in love with me instantly and I did the same with her. I was initially scared to open up because she's been through so much that I didn't know what to do or how to react to certain situations, but because her energy was contagious, I couldn't hold back. She's always happy and outgoing—it's hard not to feel the same way around her.

Her father being gone has made things more difficult for me. It's not like he was a deadbeat and left her, nor did he abuse her or wrong her in any way. If he *had* done any of those things, then she'd be able to hate him, but at least she would have closure and be able to move on. But he was taken from her. That makes the thought of him traumatizing for her.

As much as I think about what I should do for her, I don't know what to do. As her present-day father, I try to comfort her and give her unconditional love but also be strict and discipline her behavior. Raising a daughter is so much different than raising a boy! With a girl, I can't be aggressive and raw—I have to be understanding and compassionate. It's hard because I know the world is a hard and unfair place. On one hand, if I'm not hard on her, then I'm not preparing her for the world or helping her become strong enough to get through anything the world might throw at her. On the other hand, if I push too hard, I could hurt her by making her feel terrified of everything.

I need to find a balance, but I feel like nothing is right. Even when I plan everything out in my head first, something still goes wrong. And the teenage years will be coming up soon! That scares me. Dealing with boys and school is one thing, but I know the day will come when she gets mad at me and tells me "You're not my father!" That scares me. I can handle everything else, but *that* is something I will never be ready for.

I've seen that happen countless times on television and in real life. Even though it wasn't happening to me, I still felt the pain of it. Now that I'm in the same situation, it's on my mind every day. I can't get it out of my head. As many times as I've thought about it, I still don't know how I would or how I'm supposed to respond to that. If she does say that, I can't get mad at her, because it's true—I'm not. I know it's going to hurt and shatter my heart, but I can't just walk away. I can't shut down and not talk to her. Love is unconditional. I'll have to eat that and give her the same love as if it never happened and those words were never spoken. But mentally, I'm going to be broken.

With my son, I know we'll bump heads a lot because he's hard-headed and stubborn just like me. He has my attitude and my aggression and he's impulsive just like I used to be when I was a child.

Even with all that, though, I still feel like it'll be somewhat easier than raising a daughter. I can teach a boy how to be a man, but how am I supposed to teach a girl how to be a woman?

I'm going to make mistakes with both of them, and I accept that. I will never give up on them. The hardest part will be learning a way to go about teaching them that resonates. With my son, I know I can be hard on him. I have to be. I'm still going to be loving and compassionate, but I don't want him to make the same mistakes I did. I didn't have a father growing up, so I had to learn and do what I thought was right on my own. I did things even though I knew they were wrong. That way of thinking cost me my freedom and many years of my life that I'll never get back. And on top of that, because of my past, I'm worried I'll never be good enough.

I don't know what I'm supposed to do, but I do know this: I refuse to ever let myself be considered just somebody's baby daddy or a deadbeat dad. Those stereotypes are already put on every felon and Black man. When my son was born, a lady came into the room with the birth certificate for us to sign. She told us she'd be right back because she had forgotten something. Then, she looked directly at me and asked if I was still going to be there when she came back, or if I was leaving.

I didn't even know how to respond to that. I became angry and hurt at the same time. She clearly assumed that I was going to walk out of my son's life and not even be there to sign his birth certificate!! That moment replays in my mind every single day, and it still hurts like it did on the day it happened. I may not be the best father, but leaving is *never* an option or even a thought! I am a father, a provider, a protector, a role model, and everything else that comes with it. Being a father is the best thing that ever happened to me and I love every moment of it!

That said, I'll admit that having grown up without anyone to look up to has made things difficult for me—I've had no guidance when it comes to being a father. All I know is that I have to win. I have to show my kids that they can be successful. I *have* to.

Relationships

When it comes to relationships, I don't think I was meant to be in one. I really do try, and I have good intentions, but it never seems to work. Balance has never been one of my strengths; I believe that's a major cause of why I'm not good with relationships. It's not about cheating or being afraid of commitment—neither of those things are on my mind. Women have told me all my life that they love and admire my work ethic. All I know how to do is work. Especially now that I have kids!

I feel like anything can happen to me at any time. Then what? Will I have left behind a legacy or done anything in my life worth remembering? Will I have made any kind of difference in the world or done anything to make my kids proud of me? Or maybe I'll just be forgotten once I'm gone.

All I do is work and push myself. I'm either working or with my kids. Sometimes, I'm doing both at the same time. Because of that continuous focus and my fear of not being a good father, my relationships suffer because I can't find a healthy balance. I understand that when you take energy and put it into something, you're taking energy away from somewhere else. I don't purposely choose to take away from my relationships; it just seems to always happen that way.

I try to make sure all the bills and everything are covered, and I try to have some extra on the side so we can experience and do fun things as a family. In my head, I'm trying to give us the best life possible, but still, I know the little things are being overlooked. I can see that, but I don't know how to change it. I feel like if I stop or even just try to slow down, I'll fall behind on everything and won't be able to give my family the life they deserve.

The downside of all that work is neglecting my relationships. The stress and arguments don't help, either. That makes me shut down and pushes me away; it gets to the point where I want to work *more* just to be away from home. Being the man in a relationship, the fights always come down to the same thing: I'm wrong or I'm not doing something right. Even when I'm right and I make perfect sense (at least to myself), I'm wrong. I don't know if that's just how relationships are or if I'm just in the wrong relationship. The love is there, but I don't know how I'm supposed to fix myself to be a better man. Everything I've been doing in life I've *been* doing to make me a better man. Is all of that not enough?

Childhood Struggles

It started when I was younger—I would always think to myself, "Am I not wanted? Did I do something to make my father leave?" I was too young to understand why that had happened—why *any*thing happened—and my sadness turned into anger. If I wasn't good enough for my father, then how could I be good enough for anything or anyone?

I was the man of the house and I wanted to be rich so that my mom would never have to work again. But getting a job wasn't enough—minimum wage barely covers one or two bills, and when you're under 18, you can only work a certain number of hours. My only other option was the streets. Or at least, I thought that was my only option. I wasn't smart enough to notice the signs telling me that life on the streets wasn't the life for me.

All through school, sports were my biggest passion, especially football. I had dreams of playing in the NFL. I loved playing and had an extreme amount of talent: I was fast and elusive, I could tackle, and I wanted to play every position. No matter what position I was playing I gave my all. It was hard work, but it was fun. I loved every moment of it! The adrenaline flowing through my veins was electrifying.

Throughout middle and high school, I set records as a running back and I was on special teams. Football was a huge confidence booster and kept me out of trouble, at least for the most part. I'm very competitive and I have a short temper, which got me into a few physical altercations on the field. I fed into the trash talk instead of ignoring it and staying focused on the game. I was repeatedly told that I wasn't tall enough to play any sports professionally and that I would never make any team past high school.

After a while, I realized that those warnings were probably true and I gave up on my dream. With sports out of the picture, nothing was keeping me out of trouble. I was spending more time in the streets and digging a deeper hole for myself. I stopped thinking about my future and started to believe that I wouldn't live to see my 21st birthday. My entire outlook on life changed.

Traumatic Events

Being in prison was hitting rock bottom—it was one of the darkest periods of my life. The idea of prison is rehabilitation, but the reality of it is totally different. You're caged and treated like an animal, beaten down mentally and physically until you break. You're locked in a place full of people who have committed all different kinds of crimes. Some are worse than others, some are sick and unforgivable and you might be put in a room to live with one of them.

Prison is a place where you are truly alone and tested constantly. Every day for six years, I was told I'd never be good enough for anything other than occupying a prison cell. For a while, I didn't let that affect me, but eventually, those negative statements started to trigger the depression I'd already been struggling with. The experience is one of the reasons why I question everything. I'm always second-guessing myself and my decisions.

The first time I was stabbed, it caught me off guard; it took me a few minutes to even process what had just happened. I was 13 years old and on probation. My father had found out that I was in the streets and wanted to show me what they were really like. He picked me up and drove me through each of the worst neighborhoods in the city, then made me get out of the car in the Northend section of the city and told me he'd pick me up once I'd made it walking to the Southend.

It was dark and cold outside. I remember I was wearing my Miami Hurricanes Starter pullover coat. I put my hood up and started walking. The whole walk, I was cussing him out in my head and thinking about why my mom had to call him. He had never been in my life before, but now he wanted to pick me up and make me walk through the worst parts of the city.

I was too mad to be scared and so deep in my thoughts that I didn't even think about the walk itself. I made it to a McDonald's in the Southend where he picked me up. As we were driving away, I wasn't paying attention to anything he was saying—I just rolled the window down and stared out of it.

Suddenly, I felt a pressure push against my face. It felt like I'd been hit with a brick. I yelled, grabbed my face, and pulled a can opener out of my chin. Blood was leaking all over my coat and onto my lap.

I yelled at my father to pull over, and when he did, I jumped out of the car with the can opener gripped tightly in my hand. I saw a group of kids and instantly started running towards them. My impulses could've gotten me killed that day, but I was lucky—the kids got scared and ran off. Maybe they thought I had a gun or I was crazy…who knows what could've happened if things had gone differently?

When I got back into the car, my dad wanted to drive me to the hospital. I refused—I didn't like hospitals. I remember telling him to take me home and then putting a Band-Aid on my chin. I didn't feel any pain until the next morning when my adrenaline level finally went down. I still can't tell if it was a traumatic experience because I don't think I've ever fully processed what happened. But I *have* always blamed my father for it happening to begin with. Being older, I don't think blaming someone else is healthy but how would I blame myself in this case?

Passion For Writing

All my life, music has been a passion of mine—I've always loved writing and recording. It's therapeutic and has been the only way I've known how to express myself. My songs have always gotten a lot of love and respect, so I know they're good. Doing shows and shooting music videos is fun and an incredible experience. I've accomplished things I had never even dreamed of! (Aside from becoming rich and famous from my music.) Having had the opportunity to record songs with artists I grew up listening to and looked up to has been a blessing. My songs have been played on different radio stations across the country and even on a few overseas stations. When people would approach me rapping my lyrics, I couldn't believe it. All the hard work I was putting in was paying off…and I loved every moment of it!

But then something changed—the music was shifting, and rap didn't sound like rap anymore. It no longer fit me; I felt like I couldn't change with it to keep up. Depression started to kick in around that same time, and I also began to question myself more often. I would record songs and then ask myself if they were good enough. Would anyone even like them? Would the radio stations play them anymore? Then the questions started turning into statements, like "Those songs aren't good enough—no one's going to like them or buy my new album" and " I'm just wasting my time, energy, and money. I'll never be good enough to compete with the new music that's out!" and "I'm in my thirties—I'm too old to get famous. On top of that, I have a kid on the way, and I can't leave my girl at home while I go out and chase a dream." After all, we were already having issues because we weren't spending enough time together. Eventually, those thoughts caused me to lose my passion for music. I stopped recording and writing altogether.

After giving up on my music, I started working at a behavioral school in the hopes that I could stop kids from making the same mistakes I've made. I was a product of the path those kids were heading down—they didn't have nor want any guidance. They were lost.

I've always wondered why schools don't teach life skills or the consequences of actions. I think so many kids would benefit from that! And while I'd love to teach them those skills and consequences, given my anxiety, I've never really been a good speaker. So I decided to write a book. Not only for them but for my own kids as well. If something ever happens to me, then they'll have something more than just pictures, and memories of me—they'll have life lessons and they'll understand what their father was like. I was excited about my book; I knew it would have a powerful impact if I could get it into the right hands.

I treated my book-writings like it was my music. I didn't know anything about being an author, no, but I know all about being an artist! Ever since I was young, I've always known how to hustle. Once my book was published, I used that skill to my advantage and hit the streets. Every weekend I went to a different city or state with boxes of my book. I went to radio stations and different events they were hosting in order to expand my network. I stood outside of bookstores and libraries catching people who came in and out convincing them of why they *needed* to read my book. I went to Times Square which was a scary place! It was so fast-paced that it was difficult to sell books or even talk to anyone. People didn't stop, so it was hard to explain my vision.

I started to question if my book was good enough. Or was *I* good enough? What was I doing wrong? I'd been so successful—why would things change now? That was a turning point for me.

I brought a book into school for one of my students who'd been on my mind while I was writing the book. Then later that day, I was pulled aside and told I couldn't give my book to any students or even talk to them about it. Some people felt that I was glorifying prison and life in the streets. I didn't know how to respond—the only thing I glorified in Both Sides of the Street: Choices & Consequences was that even despite all of your mistakes, you can still be successful. Mistakes should never be glorified but what you learn from them is something to be proud of.

Of course, they never even opened the book or gave it a chance. Still, I wasn't going to be allowed to share the book with the people I had written it for. If someone else who hadn't been in prison had written this book, it would have been okay, but since I had written it, and I'm an ex-felon, I'm not allowed to talk about it.

Seems like no matter what a problem may be, it always comes back to me not being good enough. I'm not an author or a therapist, so I can't write a book or talk about certain topics. There are millions of personal trainers, so what makes me stand out and be good enough to train anyone? I'm a failure. Everything I do is going to fail. A felon will never be successful in life. No matter what I do, it's never enough.

Drowning In The Darkness

I spend a lot of time in my head, which is good when I'm focused and aiming for a goal. But then sometimes I get too deep in my head and depression takes over. Once that happens, there's nothing I can do to break out of it. Talking doesn't help. I can't push it down and try to bottle it up. I've tried distracting myself by focusing on other things, but that rarely works.

Most of the time, I'm stuck and I just have to wait it out. It could take days, weeks, or even months. I lose all control of my mind at that point—it's like I take a back seat to my own thoughts. Medication doesn't fix anything, and besides, I wouldn't want to stay drugged up all of the time. Masking the problem isn't helping me overcome it. I need a real solution, but it seems like that's an impossible option.

I've noticed depression affects everyone differently. The results are always the same but the cause of it, I guess, differs based on one's life and trauma. I've never been suicidal or wanted to hurt myself. Never felt like giving up, or life being too hard. Mine has been the opposite. Ever since my son was born, my outlook on life changed once again. Which also caused my depression to change as well. I've always struggled with nothing I do ever being good enough, or me not being good enough. I've struggled with the nightmares and paranoia of someone out to kill me. Believing my demons would catch up with me and it's not a fight I will be able to win. But now, after having my son and everything changing, I care about life more than I used to. I was reckless before. Consumed by the streets—I didn't care about anything or anyone.

The more I become lost in my thoughts, the more I become disconnected from reality. A lot of times, I get fixated on death. Not on *wanting* to die, but on actually dying. I think, "What would happen if I died?" That's where a majority of my questions come from. Like, who would look after my mom if I died? Who would take care of my family? I'm supposed to provide for them and protect them. If I die, I won't be able to do that or see my kids grow up. I won't be here whenever they need me or they just want to talk to their dad. What if they forget about me and their memories of me fade away as life moves on? What legacy am I leaving for my kids so they can have more than just memories and pictures? Am I a good enough father? Will they grow to resent me for not being here if I die? Would they visit me to sit and converse with me or spend time next to me?

Dying would mean missing out on so much! Life is short and unpredictable, and every day I wake up is a blessing. But although I love my life, I isolate myself by pushing everyone away. I don't try to do it purposely—I guess it's a natural reaction. I've seen so much death…I know that at any moment, I can be next.

Some days are more manageable than others, but none of these days are good days. Sometimes, I don't even want to leave my house or talk to anyone—I just want to sit in the dark in my room and be left alone. Other times, I lock myself in the bathroom or sit in the shower for an hour or more just to be alone. Hoping the water would wash away the pain of all my thoughts, but it never did. I start to cry and then get mad at myself for it because I know crying doesn't solve anything. It won't make anything better or take away these thoughts and feelings. It won't make me happy or help me understand what's wrong with me.

I just feel dead inside, like my mind and body are disconnected. That's why I always have a blank, emotionless expression. Someone could be having a conversation with me and we'll be making eye contact, but mentally, I won't even be there—instead, my mind will be shut down, still fixated on everything that's going through my head.

It's scary how good I've gotten at pretending to be engaged in a conversation. Maybe that stems from my ADD. I have a hard time focusing and paying attention unless a topic piques my interest. That's when I either become hyper-focused or depression takes over and I lose all control of my thoughts.

There are good and bad aspects of ADD just as there are with anything, so I don't consider ADD to be a disability. When I become focused on a project or I'm working on something I'm passionate about, ADD fuels my hunger and drives my motivation. At that moment, nothing else matters except achieving my goal. No matter how long it takes, I *will* remain focused on that goal.

And actually, ADD is the only thing that overpowers my depression. If I'm focused and working on a goal, then depression is blocked out of my mind and so is all other negativity. However, if I'm already struggling with depression, then there's nothing I can do because it's already too late—I can't change my thoughts to anything positive or set any goals to focus on because all of the negativity takes over and consumes my mind.

One of the worst things about battling depression is not knowing how long it will last or how severe it will be. At times it only lasts for a day or two and then I randomly snap out of it. That rarely ever happens, though—I'm usually not that lucky. When depression hits me, it generally ranges from anywhere between a week to a few months. I call those periods "cycles" because they continuously happen. Some cycles are worse than others. Still, they all cause permanent damage. Not physically, but they leave emotional scars. All of those thoughts are seared into my brain and can never be forgotten.

Having the same thoughts over and over for weeks or months on end takes a toll on you. It's mentally draining; I never feel the same afterward. Some of the thoughts are so vivid and detailed that they make my mind start to believe that they're real. When I start believing *that* is when I fall deeper into the darkness, making it harder to get out. It's like I'm drowning—the more I try to swim upward—the faster I sink. I guess that would make it more like quicksand.

I see that depression affects people in so many different ways…but then again, it affects everyone the same way in that sense. Depression breaks a person down on every level. For me, depression also makes me want to isolate myself. It happens involuntarily. I don't even realize I'm shutting down and pushing people away until after the cycle ends and I'm trying to get back to my normal daily routines. That's how I got the nickname of Ghost—I would disappear for periods of time and no one would know what had happened to me. No one would ever check on me, either, so that caused me to put up a wall and distance myself even more from everyone. Maybe that's why I'm always so emotionless. But all of this is just my experience with depression and how it affects me.

It's scary seeing how depression can make people hate themselves so much that they take their own lives. Whatever is going on in their mind is so bad that they don't want to live anymore. They give up on themselves, their lives, their families, and everything they've ever cared about. I wish something could be done to show them that yes, there are things worth living for. Life isn't always going to be pretty or easy but it *will* get better if you work hard enough to make it better.

I can't imagine that kind of hurt, but I do know that when someone's mind is made up, it's nearly impossible to change it. That kind of depression scares me the most because it affects me in such an opposite way. I don't want to die! Ever since I was released from prison, I've seen the glass as being half-full instead of half-empty. I've found reasons to live and appreciate life more. Now the thought of losing all those things terrifies me. I still have so much more life to live and things I want to do! I want to watch my kids grow up and have kids of their own. The thought of dying gives me anxiety and stresses me to the point where I can't function. I get so cautious and paranoid that I'm always looking over my shoulder like I'm still running the streets.

Although this isn't the case for me, I've also seen depression cause people to cut or burn themselves. That feeling of pain brings them comfort. I don't think I'll ever understand how physical pain can make someone feel better...but then again, I did cover my body with tattoos because they made me feel better about myself. I never realized that until I'd become addicted to wanting more; I eventually became a canvas. Tattoos seemed cool because of the artwork. Then someone pointed out that some people get tattoos more because of how getting them feels and less for the tattoos themselves. They crave the pain of a needle puncturing their skin.

Still, despite having so many tattoos, even the thought of hurting myself scares me and triggers my depression. I used to believe I could avoid that by drowning my thoughts with alcohol—I figured that as long as I was intoxicated, I wouldn't be able to think about anything. But alcohol quickly became an addiction, and instead of solving any of my many problems, it just became another one of the many I already have.

At first, drinking was comforting—it helped me to relax instead of overthinking everything. But what started as an occasional thing to do whenever I started having depressing thoughts turned into an everyday necessity. I thought I had everything under control, but really, I was in a losing battle with my independence.

I had never imagined that would ever happen to me! I refused to let myself believe that I could be beaten and *not* be in control of myself or my actions. Maybe it was pride or my ego that caused me to ignore all the warning signs. I still couldn't look in the mirror and *not* see all the bad things I'd done. I still couldn't block out all the thoughts of depression that I was trying to avoid. Everything was still there—drinking just highlighted my problems and made me hate myself more.

It took years of battling addiction to finally overcome it. It wasn't easy, because before I could even start on the road to recovery, I had to admit to myself that I had a problem. For a long time, I refused to believe that I had a problem, or that I could be addicted to anything. Depression was in control and I didn't even realize it.

As much as the thought of death scares me, the only way I would want to die is if I developed Dementia. I don't want to die, no, but I don't want to live like that, either. It runs in my family and that scares me to death; it scares me *more* than death. The thought of looking into my kid's faces and not knowing who they are is terrifying. I wouldn't be able to understand what's going on at that point or have any control over it. I would never want to put them through that!

Even though they would want to keep me around as long as possible I wouldn't want them to see me or remember me like that. Maybe that's selfish on my part, but if I ever can't remember who my kids are, I don't want to live anymore. Ever since my grandmother died, those thoughts have been on my mind. Seeing her like that wasn't easy, and my son was too young to understand what was happening. He was just scared. I didn't know how to explain Dementia to a two-year-old. That made me start thinking about dementia happening to me, which added to my depression.

I don't know how to beat depression or if it even can be beaten. Every day I just try my best to manage it and accept that it's a part of me. I've always been optimistic and able to overcome many obstacles in my life but depression is different. I've been struggling with it for my entire life. Even when I think I've made some type of progress, it pops up to laugh in my face and remind me that it can take over anytime it wants. There's nothing I can do to stop it.

Anxiety Takes Over

Whenever I get nervous or feel uncomfortable, I start sweating. It becomes visible; it drips down my face and my body feels like it's overheating. Then once the anxiety sets in, I start stuttering. My chest feels tight, and my breathing gets heavy. It feels like I'm having a panic attack—my mind starts racing and I can't focus on anything. That mainly happens whenever I'm around new people or a large group of people. I shut down and become awkward. I don't know how to handle these situations, so I just stay quiet and start fidgeting.

In a large crowd, I feel like everyone is watching me, even staring at me. I become paranoid and dysregulated; I start constantly checking my pockets, making sure I have everything; I feel as if someone is going to reach into my pockets and steal something. I watch everyone because I feel like someone is going to sneak up on me and hit me or stab me. I have to be mindful and always be a step ahead of everyone else. All it takes is one mistake—one slip-up could cost me my life.

My awareness shoots all the way up and I don't know how to turn it down. Being in large crowds always causes this reaction. It doesn't matter where I am or who I'm with—I could be at a concert or a sports event or on vacation and still feel this way. Sometimes that takes away the enjoyment of being at any of these places and I can't even allow myself to have fun. When I go somewhere with my kids and I feel anxious, it's like all my focus shifts directly onto them and I don't pay attention to anything or anyone else. They become my crutch. I know that's not good for them and I hate that they see me like that. Fortunately, I don't think they realize what's happening. I pray they'll never pick up that trait from me. I want them to be more outgoing and social than I am, but it's hard for me to model having those attributes. On top of all that, I don't want them to grow up with attachment issues because of me. They don't deserve that.

When it comes to meeting new people, I get anxious and nervous. I can't help sizing them up and giving off a vibe that seems unwelcoming and unfriendly. I've done so many bad things to so many people when I was younger that meeting someone new makes me paranoid—I stare at them and wonder if I ever hurt them or anyone close to them. Is karma catching up with me? If they look familiar in any way or if they say that *I* look familiar, I immediately get defensive—I assume I look familiar because of something negative I did, never mind that I've also done a lot of positive things for a lot of people.

Initial conversations aren't even about me getting to know the other person, they're about me trying to figure out where their head is at and if they have any ill intentions. It takes a while before I actually open up to anyone if I ever do at all. I have major trust issues, and that makes it hard for me to want to be social. I've become comfortable with being anti-social and alone. Being alone is like a safe space for me; I prefer it over having company. Awkward small talk makes me feel so bothered and uncomfortable that I'll just stand there in silence or pull out my phone and act like I'm doing something important instead of initiating a conversation. I don't know how to have small talk, or what to say. I've heard a quote from Tom Hardy that gives me chills every time I hear it because it's so relatable: "Being alone for a while is dangerous. It's addicting. Once you see how peaceful it is, you don't want to deal with people anymore."

Another thing that gives me anxiety is waiting. I hate waiting! Knowing that something is going to happen and having to wait for it is unsettling. My mind starts racing and I become hyper-fixated. Patience is a weakness I've always struggled with because of my anger issues. I thought I was getting better with it for a while until a situation arose where my patience was tested. Waiting feels like torture! My mind begins to think about every possible outcome and all the different things I could do to make the best out of the situation even though it won't matter what I do. I do not affect the outcome. Still, I can't stop obsessing over it. I know obsessing only makes things worse and adds more stress on top of everything else I'm already dealing with, but knowing the truth doesn't stop my mind from racing.

But despite its negative effects, I don't know if I would be the same person without the anxiety. As much as I hate having it, it's made me who I am today. I feel like it's also had an impact on many other things, like my OCD. That's yet another one of the many disorders I battle. For as long as I can remember, OCD has affected me. I would catch myself counting squares whenever I walked into a room with tiled floors or counting each step any time I went up or down stairs. It took a while before I realized I was even doing that. Like, whenever I would knock on a door, I had to knock three times. I tried to switch it up and knock less or more, but when I would knock less, I'd have to finish until I got to three, and if I knocked more, I'd pause for a second and knock again three times as if I was restarting the process. Anytime I tried to change it, I'd feel myself getting anxious and unsettled until the OCD forced me to do it again. It felt like my brain was auto-correcting my body. I never understood why it had to be the number three, and only when knocking.

Sometimes when the anxiety gets so bad that it has my mind spinning, I have to sit down. If I'm home, I lay down and curl up, hoping to slow down my thoughts. When that happens, I'm usually stuck for a while. I try to focus on one thing, but the anxiety is so loud in my head that I can't always manage to focus on just one thing. That's usually when I get migraines. I don't get them often, thankfully, but I've learned what triggers them.

I haven't learned any coping skills for anxiety. I don't know if there are any...Maybe I haven't looked in the right places or found the right kind of help, but *is* there even a cure for anxiety? I don't believe there is a cure, so I don't allow myself to get my hopes up. I'm not a scientist, or a doctor, or anyone on a level to know what cures there are. All I know is, that I've never seen anyone be cured of it. The only thing I've ever seen or heard were tips on how to deal with it while it's happening but that's never guaranteed. And besides, everyone is different—what works for one person isn't going to work for everyone else. I just try my best to focus my time and attention on things that I *do* have control over. It's like that saying "Don't cry over spilled milk." Why should I stress over anything I can't change? That would be pointless—it wouldn't change anything.

I wish I could get rid of my anxiety. I wish I didn't have to feel like this all the time—I wish I weren't always angry and paranoid. It's bad enough that I'm short-tempered and everything irritates me. Once my anxiety kicks in, then I become frustrated, too. When I was younger, I would always get into fights because of that. I didn't know what anxiety was or how to channel my anger, and not knowing caused me to use my hands instead of words anytime I got into an altercation. That's a big part of why I spent my entire pre-teen and teenage years in and out of court and on probation. Now that I'm older, even though I still feel those same urges, I know I can't go around putting my hands on everyone who gets me mad. That's not healthy, and besides, I could end up back in prison—which is a place I never want to go back to again.

Having anger issues is dangerous. It's why I've been stabbed a few times. I didn't know how to let things go and just walk away, and that's how situations escalate and bad things happen. Once things escalate to that point, it's too late to calm down. There's no talking or trying to reason with me. I don't care about what obstacles are in my way when my back is against the wall. The only way I can go is forward. That's a scary feeling.

Anxiety can trigger so many other things I have no control over. I think what stresses me out the most is knowing the anxiety can hit at any moment and there's nothing I can do about it. At least I've become a lot better with my anger issues physically—instead of expressing my anger violently the way I used to, I internalize it. That isn't healthy, either, but what can I do if neither option is a good one? I'm either hurting others or I'm hurting myself. I don't see either choice being a true solution, but I do know that I don't want to hurt others anymore. I just want to better myself so that I can better my future.

The Stress Is Real

I really believe that stress will be the death of me. I'm always stressed out! Mostly it's my fault for putting so much on my plate and trying to manage it all. I know I can't do everything all at once, but I refuse to let that stop me from reaching my goals. Even though it's draining and very stressful, what kind of man would I be if I just gave up? I feel like I'm the definition of the expression "I'm gonna ride until the wheels fall off."

I noticed my first white hair when I was twenty-one years old. Since I exceeded my life expectancy it seems like I got white hair instead. I'd been stressing myself out for so long that it had become physically noticeable! I started shaving my hair off to avoid seeing the white hair. Dyeing my hair seemed like too much of a hassle. I'd always kept my hair short, so it didn't bother me to take it all the way off.

Then I started getting white hairs on my beard. That's when it hit me: I really needed to slow down. I was stressing myself out too much. I love my beard and I've had it so long that I feel like I'd look weird without it. I also realize there's nothing I can do to completely stop getting white hairs—I'm only trying to delay the inevitable.

The truth is, time doesn't stop for anyone or anything. Bills won't wait for you while you're sick or on vacation or taking a mental health day. Nobody cares what your reasons or excuses are once you've passed your due date. I refuse to ever allow myself to be in that situation. I don't want to be behind! I don't want to live check to check! I don't ever want to struggle again the way I struggled when I was growing up.

I'm going to work until I'm not only comfortable but ahead. I have a goal number that I want to maintain—that's my baseline, my zero. I want to stay well above that number so that if anything ever were to happen, I could still be comfortable until I got myself back on my feet. But that kind of mindset is bound to be accompanied by stress. There's no way to stop it. Just as money can't buy happiness, it doesn't solve stress. If you have money, then you've dealt with the stress of making it and everything else along the way. If you don't have it, how are you going to eat? How are you going to pay bills? Where are you going to sleep or live? I don't know any way around stress. I know ways of distracting yourself from it, but those are only temporary fixes, not a real solution.

Stress is a major cause of the headaches I get and the reason why my blood pressure has been high over the past few years. I didn't realize it was that bad until I went to the doctor and had to start taking medication for high blood pressure. I'd also put on weight that I hadn't even noticed I was putting on. Once I stepped onto that scale, I felt embarrassed. I had never weighed that much before! I was feeling heavier and out of shape, but physically, I hadn't seen it.

Looking at the numbers on the scale hit hard; I felt depression beginning to take over. How was I going to lose weight if I kept stress-eating? How was I supposed to manage always being stressed out and depressed? I still have to show up to work every day and take care of my family. I don't ever want my family to be stressed, so I battle my own stress in silence. I want my family to have the life they want and deserve. No matter what the price for that is, I have to make it happen. No excuses. There's no way I could look into my kids' eyes and tell them that they can't do or have something I could have provided if I had just worked a little bit harder. That would never sit well with me.

Aside from money issues, I struggle with deadlines. Even when I know I've gotten everything done or I did everything right, I still stress about the fact that a deadline is approaching. I'm always thinking that maybe I'm missing something or didn't do something right or that maybe I could have done something better. Those thoughts take over my mind until the deadline has passed and I can move on. My mind will take the littlest things and blow them up until they're the only things I can think about. I can't focus on anything else. I become obsessed, and even though I know how stressful that obsession is, my mind won't stop thinking about whatever I'm fixated on. Just like my anxiety or depression, I have no control over that kind of obsession.

Slowly, though, I've been finding little ways to get better at managing the stress. When it comes to bills, I pay them off early and get them out of the way so that I don't have to worry about them. Plus, then I'm ahead. Otherwise, when things get busy, I might forget due dates. Then, I'd be late and have another issue to deal with.

Insecurity plays a big role in my stress because I always overthink things and question myself. I never know if I'm doing anything right, and I feel like I'm always getting negative attention because of that. Anything I do or any thought I have, I question. Even when I know I'm good at doing something, I still doubt myself.

I wish I could be like so many other people who live carelessly, but I can't. I have too many responsibilities and priorities to be careless. If I slip up or slack off one time, it could have a ripple effect—then, it would take all of my time and energy just to get back to where I was. How is that supposed to help me get ahead? I feel like I *have* to overthink everything. I *have* to stress. And if I can't handle stress, then I'm going to break anytime I'm under pressure. I can't allow that to happen when I have people who depend on me.

At times, I get so stressed out that I just want to scream and start breaking everything. I know I can't do that, though. Breaking things will only add to the stress I'm already dealing with. Think about it, I'd have to clean it all up, and I might have broken something I worked hard for or needed. How does that help me? Having a mental breakdown would only put me into a state where I can't function, and that isn't going to help me do what needs to get done or take any of this stress off my plate.

The goal is to minimize stress since I know I can't eliminate it altogether. Solve one problem, and another one arises. If you don't solve the first problem fast enough, more start piling up; eventually, you become overwhelmed. Having so many things to stress about makes it hard to focus on one thing at a time. On top of that, having ADD makes it hard to focus on *anything*. I have a short window before my mind shifts to something else. It's like I'm getting hit from every direction, with yet another thing to stress about. I don't understand how people can procrastinate until the last minute and be okay with it. That would drive me insane! It bothers me seeing other people do it.

One of the most stressful things is the pressure of grinding. For example, when I make music or write a book, after I've finished composing or writing and the product is done, that's when the grind begins. I've never had a company or a team of people working for me, so everything I've done, I've done it myself. Yeah, I feel a sense of relief that I've accomplished my goal. But then isn't about me anymore—I'm pushing my product out to the public and I have to worry about how they'll view me and react to it.

I have thought about what it would be like if I had a company or a team behind me helping me, but I don't. So I'm only be wasting my time and energy thinking about "What if?" I'm okay with grinding alone. It makes me respect and appreciate the hustle. It keeps me humble.

Of course, I want every album and every book to be successful. That would be a dream come true, but then reality hits. I don't have a budget for marketing to extend my reach all over the world. I have kids. I have to be at work. I have a mortgage and many other bills. I have to find ways to make it work, or else everything I've done will be for nothing.

I've always struggled with the question "How am I going to do this?" until I stopped asking that question and started asking "What am I going to do today?" Neither question mitigates the level of stress I'm dealing with, but at least I'm not stressing about the "*how*" anymore. Grinding is all day, every day. It's never-ending. Grinding is dedication and hard work; it's a lifestyle that's not for everybody. You have to have it in you.

Sometimes I have to think about what I'll do if I find an out-of-town event that could benefit me but that coincides with work. On top of that, I have my kids to consider. What am I going to do? Am I going to miss out on that opportunity?

You better believe I will be in the car and at that event *with* my kids, promoting my book or whatever it is I'm promoting! I'll be stressing every minute that goes by because I know I have to get back to town to drop the kids off and get to work on time, but I *will* make it happen. I only have small windows of opportunity. They may not be big enough to climb through, but I will definitely stress myself out trying to find ways to reach through that window before it closes.

There's no win-win scenario dealing with stress because there's no avoiding it. As bad as that sounds, I accept it and find relief in my accomplishments. I appreciate each win no matter how small it is before I move on to whatever is next. It's like an endless loop of one thing after another.

I'm never content with just reaching my goal. A goal isn't a destination or an end point to me—it's a checkpoint. If I don't see it that way, then what would I do after I've accomplished my goal? What would be next?

Unanswered Questions

They say the only thing certain in life is death. There's no understanding of how, why, or when it's going to happen, but it's going to happen. Everything else about life is uncertain and I don't think *I'll* ever understand it. I know I can't even figure out *my* own life! Being diagnosed with various disorders like there's something wrong with me and being looked at like I'm mentally unstable has made me feel like I really might be. After being told all my life that I have problems, how am I supposed to believe that I *don't*?

As a kid, I was told to "man up." People always said, everyone goes through things, and crying doesn't solve anything. I was taught to never show my emotions because that's a sign of weakness, and in this world, you can't afford to be weak. All I know how to do is bottle up my thoughts and feelings. Any time I *did* try to share them, they were either used against me or thrown in my face. So you can see why I'm skeptical when it comes to talking about my demons.

There's one question in particular that I struggle with the most. I always find myself thinking about it. Am I really *battling* demons or am I so far lost that I *am* the demon? I used to believe I was battling my demons but I feel like I don't know the answer to that question anymore. Have they already won and I just haven't realized it? Did I even stand a chance?

My head is filled with thoughts that I'll never understand. I've tried to ask these questions to those who seemed like they might know about these kinds of things, but I've got nothing other than hesitant and stuttered responses. I knew their answers were fake and opinion-based because the eyes never lie. Every time I ask, I can see the look on their faces as they scramble to find the words to explain what they don't know.

For a while, it was entertaining—even funny—to watch each person react the same way. At that point, I was no longer asking those questions to get answers anymore because I knew I wasn't going to *get* any real answers. I felt like my demons had taken over and the whole thing was a game to them. Or that, I had become the demon and enjoyed mocking all the professionals who claim to have all the answers.

It took years before I was able to let that game go, but one day I did. It just happened. It's like I got bored or just didn't care anymore. Either way, I stopped asking questions. At least out loud, anyway. I still ask myself if I'm a good person every day when I wake up and look in the mirror. It seems like I've lost sight of myself along the way, which isn't really surprising. Trauma changes people. When you experience so much of it, you can't expect to still be the same person as you were yesterday.

While I was incarcerated, I was forced to face all of my demons. I was in a place where I couldn't run away from them or find any of the distractions I knew. I spent the majority of my twenties in prison. My anxiety has been on a 1,000 since the day I was arraigned until after I was released and had gotten adjusted to being home again. While I was in prison, all of my thoughts were crying out how badly I wanted to go home, but in reality, I knew that wasn't an option. I couldn't escape depression; I went through countless cycles while I was there. Sitting with nothing but my thoughts all day and all night was traumatizing. I had to relive each day over and over like I was in the movie *Groundhog Day*. The days felt like they would never end, and my insecurities made me feel like my life was over. I kept thinking I was a failure and I'd never amount to anything. On top of that, being a felon, I'd forever be viewed and judged as a criminal who belongs in jail.

How am I supposed to get a job when I can't pass a background check? I'm Black, covered in tattoos, and have a violent criminal history. Two out of three of those are choices that I've made and they can't be undone. I know that's why my applications are usually overlooked or thrown away. Why do I feel like I'll never be as good as anyone else when I will outwork anyone who's put in front of me? And I know that due to my past mistakes, I'll have to work harder than anyone else just to have an opportunity to start at the bottom.

Why does a single mistake I've made outweigh all of the good I've done in my life? It seems like the odds are stacked against me and I'm supposed to fail. Or is that just another stereotype I'm trying to prove wrong? I never thought I would even make it to see twenty-one, but I did. It hasn't been an easy journey—the stress, the pain, the trauma, and everything else has taken a toll on me.

Each of the times I've been stabbed, I always asked myself if that was it. Was I going to die? Was I going to bleed out? I was scared that if I went to the hospital, they would ask questions that I couldn't answer. So going there wasn't always an option for me. I would have to clean and bandage the wound myself, the way I'd seen a doctor do it on TV, and then just hope I'd be okay.

Why can't I walk away from confrontations? Why am I so opinionated and why do I have such a hard time holding my tongue? I've always been quiet and kept to myself, but at the same time, I never back down when someone comes at me the wrong way. I'm sure that has to do with my anger issues and stubbornness. After being stabbed, I'd get even more paranoid and feel like I could get stabbed again at any moment. It made me feel vulnerable and that's scary because I have no idea how I may react in any given situation.

How can I trust anyone when the people closest to me want to see me fail? They smile in my face, but only when it's convenient for them. I've noticed that the majority of people only do things if it benefits them. They're only around when they need you but whenever *I'm* down, everyone disappears. A childhood friend from the first grade told on me and became one of the reasons why I went to prison. Where was the trust there? When I was in prison, nobody wrote to me, nobody came to visit me, nobody sent me any money orders. I was on my own. Everyone I had looked out for was gone and living their lives like I didn't exist anymore.

They say that you never really know someone until something bad happens. I truly believe that. Being locked up with killers, rapists, child molesters, and gang members when I wasn't gang-affiliated didn't make it easy for me to trust anyone.

I did meet a few good people over the years, though...and most of them died in front of me. The first time I saw that happen was one of the most traumatic experiences I've ever had because he was like a brother to me. I witnessed the whole thing. Then it happened again and again with others who became friends over the years while I was incarcerated. I started to become numb to the pain. I didn't feel anything anymore. It's like my brain didn't know how to process everything that was happening. It was too much. Before that, I had seen people die, but that hadn't had any effect on me because it wasn't anyone I knew or was close to.

I don't understand why I can't let go of all of these thoughts and the accompanying trauma. Talking about everything hasn't cleared my mind or my conscience in any way. It seems like nothing has worked for me. I've tried so many different options in the hopes that something would help, but I continue to be let down. What else can I do aside from medicating myself or doing shock therapy or hypnosis? I refuse to do any of those things; the few people I've met who did pursue those treatments weren't the same afterward. I guess that's the point, but that isn't the kind of change I'm going for. Why would I want to lose myself in the process? I love who I am and all the hard work I've done that has gotten me to where I am. Who would I be if I lost that? Is this something that can even be cured—something I can move on from—or is all this pain and trauma who I am?

I've been fighting all of my life, both physically and mentally. I will never give up, but I can feel my body and mind getting tired. I'm exhausted. My body is failing me because I've pushed it too hard when I should have taken better care of it. But what can I do now other than regret past mistakes? I can't go back and change anything. In my mind, I can still do everything I could do before, but then I try, and reality hits. Hard. That hurts. I never thought I would struggle with having limitations! I always thought and felt like I could do anything.

Like I was saying, I never expected I'd live to see twenty-one, but I did, and I appreciate every day. At least, now I do. I was reckless in my twenties. I felt like I was invincible and I could do whatever I wanted. That attitude ended up costing me six years of my life…but it may have also saved my life.

When I exceeded the stereotype of kids who lived the lifestyle I did, I was lost. I didn't know what to do anymore. I didn't have any long-term goals set for myself because I hadn't thought I needed any. Even now, thinking about the next year still seems like a lifetime away; I don't know if I'll make it, so I try not to think about the future in depth. I've been able to create and set goals for myself, but I don't put a timeframe on them. If I did, I'd never reach any of my goals—I'd be too busy stressing about whether or not I'd still be around in a year. They say tomorrow isn't promised, but I feel like I don't know if I'll even make it through *today*. There are things in my head that tell me I won't, but I try my best to block them out and make every day that I wake up a productive day.

That doesn't stop all of these questions from arising, though. Like, what am I supposed to do? How can I get these demons out of my head? Why is this happening to me? Am I going to die without ever knowing what's wrong with me?

Still, as bad as things get sometimes, I've developed a *winning* mentality. I refuse to let these demons beat me! I refuse to quit, and to *not* get back up when I'm knocked down! And I refuse to let anyone tell me that I can't do something! I'm committed to this mindset and passionate about anything I put my energy into. It took years for me to realize that failing isn't the same as losing.

Failing doesn't mean that I'm not good enough or that I can't do something. I've opened my eyes to see that failing is a learning experience—failing isn't about *if* I can or can't do something, it's about *how* I did it and *why* it didn't work. I've done so many things with no knowledge or experience that I never would've imagined I could accomplish, but I did—by having a *winning* mentality.

I'm just hoping that one day I'll be able to find a healthy balance and have peace. I hope to not let any of these demons or questions haunt me anymore. My goal is to get to a point in my life where I don't have to question or second-guess everything. A point where I don't find myself shutting down or feeling insecure anymore. A point where the nightmares stop and I can have normal dreams.

I want to stop stressing so much and enjoy my life, or at least what's left of it before it's over. That's the goal and I don't plan on giving up.

Additional Resources

988 Suicide & Crisis Lifeline

A national network of local crisis centers that provides 24/7, free and confidential support.

www.988lifeline.org

SAMHSA
Substance Abuse and Mental Health Services Administration

1-800-662-4357
www.samhsa.gov

The Hardest Choices

A network that provides group and confidential support services.

www.thehardestchoices.com

Follow the Author

On all social media platforms
@iammarcuswhitley

Previous Books

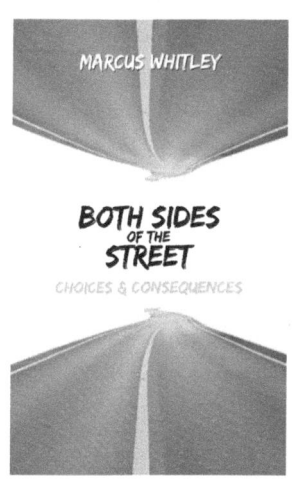

BOTH SIDES OF THE STREET:
CHOICES & CONSEQUENCES

GREATNESS UNDER
PRESSURE